Breaking Bounds

Photographs © 1992 Lois Greenfield

© 1992 Thames and Hudson Ltd, London
Reprinted 1994

ISBN 0-500-27670-6

Printed and bound in Singapore by
C.S. Graphics

1 Jamey Hampton, Ashley Roland,
  Daniel Ezralow, Sheila Lehner
  ISO DANCE COMPANY, 1990

2 Molissa Fenley
  Provenance Unknown, 1988

3–9 Gail Gilbert, David Parsons
  *Explorations on a Theme:
  Expulsion from Paradise*, 1990

1

THAMES AND HUDSON

Breaking

THE DANCE PHOTOGRAPHY

WILLIAM A. EWING

Bounds

OF Lois Greenfield

CONTENTS

INTRODUCTION

A close examination of the linkage between dance and photography suggests a paradox; for all the dance world's dependency on photography to represent its accomplishments, photography is inherently the least suited medium to do the dance justice. After all, dance is the controlled passage of bodies through time and space. The essence of the dance—and our comprehension of it—stems from the seamless interconnectedness of its movements and gestures. But photography fragments time; a single image is a vision of one moment torn from its context. And while photography fragments time, it fractures space. Its absolute universe is the frame, outside of which nothing exists. What once happened in the fullness of space is now brutally cordoned off, and what we are allowed to see is imprisoned in two dimensions.

Furthermore, photography is inherently biased towards certain aspects of dance irrespective of their significance *vis-à-vis* the whole; a spectacular leap, for example, is more photogenic than a more subtle movement which may in fact be more essential choreographically. Also highly photogenic are certain poses and attitudes, such as positions in which arms and legs are outstretched along diagonal lines. And because dance is fleeting and photography enduring, imperfect moments which are overlooked or forgiven in the rapid flux of stage performance are felt to be unacceptable in what is, after all, a lasting document. Consequently, photography is pressured to create images of perfection, the perfect point, the perfect *jetée*, the perfectly serene expression, even if this requires dozens of attempts before the camera to "get it right" (or even painting over the offending detail). This demand for technical perfection, coupled with the bias towards what is inherently photogenic, has had the effect not only of misrepresenting the dance but also of stifling photographic creativity. Thus we find many a dance archive filled with reams of flat and unconvincing imagery.

On the other hand, one cannot hold the photographers of the past entirely responsible for what were in fact severe technical limitations. Early in the 20th century dancers were sometimes held up with cables to keep them still long enough for the required exposures. Even without cables dancers were expected to hold difficult poses for uncomfortably long periods, which inevitably led to stiff results. The introduction of powerful artificial light, in particular the strobe, radically changed this situation. But a technical solution is not necessarily an esthetic solution, and artificial light was not the panacea it was expected to be. The "split second" was exactly that: a frozen moment, just as unconvincing, and often as ludicrous, as the earlier, painfully elongated pose. The depiction of movement in a fluid and believable way has been the shoal on which many a photographic enterprise has foundered. Of course it is true that a great deal was being expected of what was, after all, "still" photography. This paradox, and the dogged refusal of all

3

the Hasselblad camera, with its square picture format, and her encounter with David Parsons and Daniel Ezralow, then two young Paul Taylor dancers, who entered enthusiastically into a free-wheeling and highly experimental collaboration which has lasted to this day.

What characterizes a Lois Greenfield image? First, the obvious: a square format, bounded on four sides by the black borders which represent the camera frame. These black borders are the thin negative strips around each image which separate one shot from the next. They are included in the print for three reasons: firstly, to define the parameters of the actual composition in those cases where the backgrounds are pure white; secondly, to demonstrate the exact parameters of the image *as it was composed in the viewfinder*; and, thirdly, as a formal device to provide an active rather than passive element or force to which the dancers are seen to respond in a dynamic way—bouncing off, hanging from, breaking through. These borders therefore contain but do not entirely restrict—they are, in a sense, permeable.

It is tension, or rather tensions, between various opposing forces which empower a Greenfield image: between the force of gravity and weightlessness (see, for example, "falling", Plate 33; "floating", 62; "soaring", 32; "flying", 44); between the linear and the curvilinear (Plate 41); between attraction and repulsion (Plate 39); between vertical, diagonal, and horizontal vectors (Plate 40); between serenity of expression and taxing physical activity (Plate 1); between balance and imbalance (Plate 67); between freedom and constraint (Plate 80); between connection and disconnection (Plates 49 versus 39); between figuration and abstraction (Plate 65); and between order and chaos (Plate 66).

To propose just *how* such dynamic results are achieved is beyond the scope of this introduction, but some light may be shed on the subject by taking the briefest of looks at Greenfield's working method. What first must be made clear is how she does *not* work. There is no studio or darkroom sleight-of-hand, no cables, no hidden supports, no dancers lying on the floor in attitudes of motion with the camera directly above, no printing-in of bodies after the fact, and virtually no cropping save for the occasional image of large groups where it is a technical necessity (and intended from the outset). Nor does she have her dancers pose. Instead, she gets her dancers dancing, and, as dance critic Deborah Jowitt puts it, "snatches the image out of a field of motion."

Absolutely fundamental to her way of working is collaboration, no matter how brief the encounter with the dancer. Through mutually respectful collaboration in which both parties risk abandoning their set notions, dancer and photographer are able to push the limits of their understanding and the boundaries of their respective arts.

14

parties concerned to accept defeat, was elegantly voiced by Elizabeth McCausland when she called for dance photography to create "an image which, though it cannot move, and never can hope to move, yet will seem about to move." It is a further paradox that a brilliant resolution should be devised by a photographer for whom the dance itself is decidedly of secondary importance. But such is the achievement of Lois Greenfield.

If the allegiance of the conventional dance photographer is to the dance, with photography in the role of handmaiden—there to report on its progress, document its achievements for posterity, idealize the dance and idolize the dancer—Greenfield's allegiance is first and foremost to photography. Dance is her subject matter, or, as she puts it in the accompanying interview, her "landscape." Dance is not, however, incidental; she *needs* the trained bodies with their athletic prowess, their acquired ability to previsualize themselves in space (able to chart their trajectories and land with pinpoint accuracy), and their ability to mould their bodies into expressive forms as required. What she does *not* need is prescribed choreography: "I tell my dancers to leave their choreography at the door," says Greenfield. Her fundamental concern is with kinetic energy: energy contained, constrained, and released. Not surprisingly, the dancers with whom Greenfield works relish the freedom she gives them; surprising, perhaps, is the positive response of many of the choreographers, some of whom have discovered new aspects of their work in her imagery.

Greenfield began her career as a photo-journalist in the early 1970s, when events in the dance world were becoming increasingly newsworthy. What initially attracted her to dance photography was its relative immunity from editorial interference; unlike her political coverage, which was judged for its content rather than its form, dance photography was pure form—or, rather, the form *was* the content. With time, however, she grew increasingly disenchanted with the norms of traditional dance photography and began consciously to look for the off-peaks and off-angles that could bring a fresh vision to the dance. She also became more and more restive in performance and dress rehearsal situations in which the photographer is reduced to the status of a powerless observer, and by 1982 had obtained her own studio where she could exert something approaching total control of the event. Her rechoreography began casually and naturally enough—no more than a hand or a foot being slightly repositioned so as not to obscure a face. Eventually, however, these interventions increased to the point where she herself began to choreograph, then to where choreography was completely abandoned, and finally to the point where she choreographed herself specifically *for* the camera (that is, these "dances" can never be seen on stage). This momentous advance would never have been possible save for the convergence of two elements: her discovery of

13,14 >

15

16

17

18

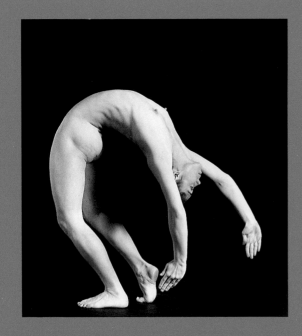

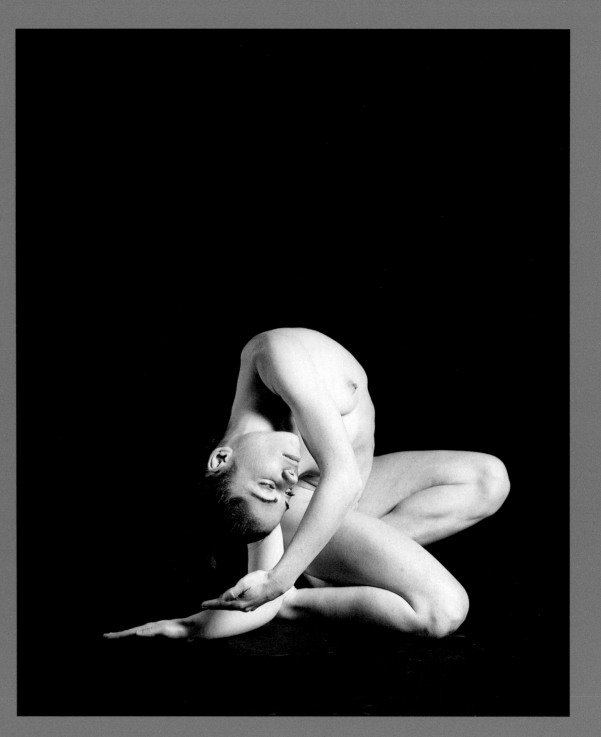

27–29

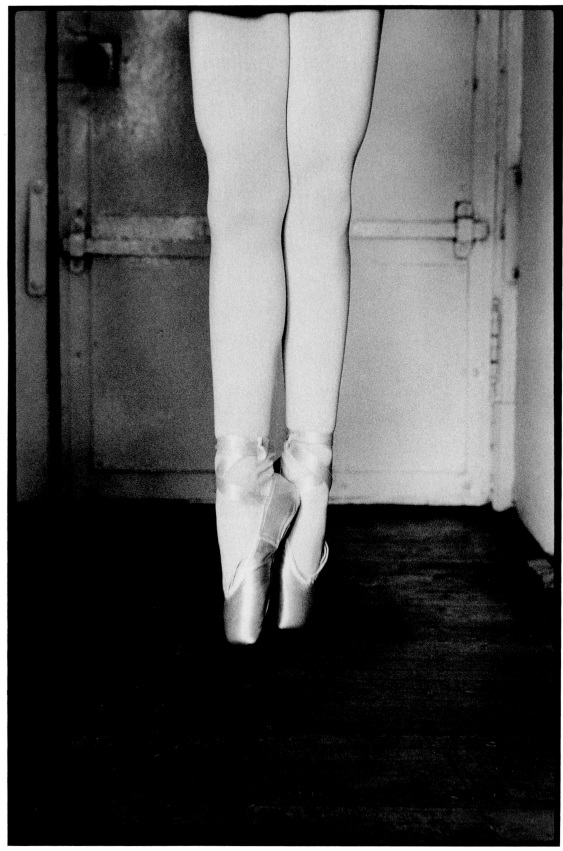

3

52

53

55

61

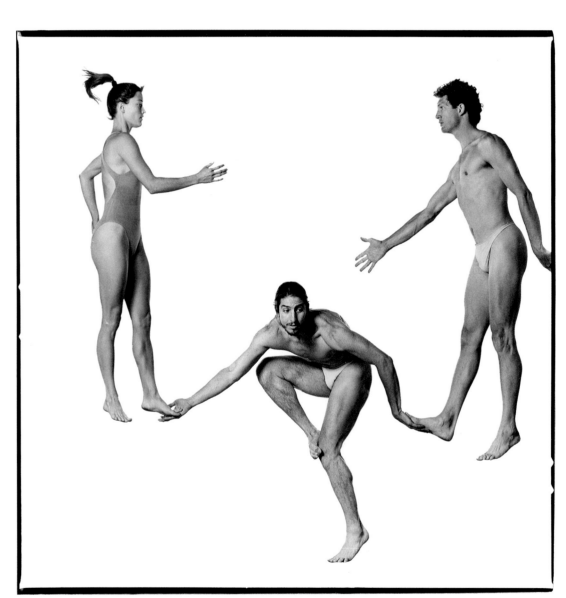

5

WAE The world perceives you as "Lois Greenfield, Dance Photographer." But this isn't a perception which does justice to your art, is it?

LG No, it isn't. In fact, being called a dance photographer makes me bristle. Of course, looked at from a literal perspective, I *am* a dance photographer in that I provide a service to the dance world by taking photographs which will be used by the various companies for posters and brochures advertising their programs, and sent to magazines and newspapers to accompany reviews. My problem is not so much being labeled "dance photographer," as accepting the assumptions that go along with the term. I've rebelled against the notion of the dance photographer as handmaiden to the dance, that is, charged with providing either a literal or an idealized transcription. Instead, I see myself as a photographer whose subject matter happens to be the dance. You might say that dance is my landscape. The root of my interest is movement, or rather how movement can be interpreted photographically. And dance provides a perfect opportunity for this.

WAE So, as a logician might say, dance is a necessary but not a sufficient condition for your interest. It's only a starting point, a platform. But before we address these ideas, I'd like to know how you came to dance photography or photography itself, for that matter, in the first place?

LG Although I'd studied anthropology at Brandeis University in Boston, which was a *very* liberal arts college, I also took some film courses and I thought I'd combine my interests by making ethnographic films. But I also took up photography on my own and by my senior year I was heavily involved in photojournalism, working for Boston's counter-cultural newspapers, covering what seemed to be a quintessentially early seventies' circus of rock stars, demonstrations and riots. I found that I liked working on my own and I decided to pursue photography instead of film for this reason. Then in 1973 I got married and moved to New York, where I discovered a whole new area—dance photography.

WAE Did you discover it, or did it discover you?

LG A bit of both. Dance was just achieving immense popularity, partly due to the success in the West of the Russian superstars: Rudolf Nureyev, Mikhail Baryshnikov, and others. It was an era of choreographic invention: ballet cross-fertilized with modern forms (Nureyev with Paul Taylor, Twyla Tharp with the American Ballet Theater, Baryshnikov with Alvin Ailey). Shortly after I began working for the *Village Voice*—my first stories were on politics and elections—my editor asked me to cover Paul Taylor rehearsing with Nureyev. It must have been the first collaboration between a ballet superstar and a major modern dance

INTERVIEW

David Parsons hovers over the sphinx-like figure of Denise Roberts. This series of images is a fine example of the improvisational and collaborative approach characteristic of Greenfield's work. Defiance of gravity is a constant theme. (See also Plate 50.)

company, but apparently no one else was interested in doing it! Then I found that other publications wanted the material as well, and I sold the photos to the *New York Times*, and thought, "Hey, there's a market here, this is a good idea." I've always been encouraged by success and when I see an opening I go with it.

It was at this time that I realized that I liked photographing the dance—both for the form and the content—though I didn't really know *how* to do it. At the same time I realized that photographing dance freed me from the responsibility of conveying information. Reportage photos inevitably "said" something, took a position on the event. My editors would always select the photo with the correct "content," rather than the one with the best lighting and composition. I didn't have to worry about that in dance photography: the form was the content!

WAE At this point, then, in the early seventies, you weren't photographing dance exclusively?

LG No, I wasn't. For example, I heard about a theater piece, *The Life and Times of Joseph Stalin*, by Robert Wilson, which was being premiered at the Brooklyn Academy of Music. Wilson was a radical theatrical innovator and I was captivated by the piece. I went out to Brooklyn almost every night to photograph it. And this material was published in *Dance Magazine*. In short order I had work published in *Time*, *Newsweek*, and *Rolling Stone*, among others. But the *Voice* work has been the cornerstone of my twenty-year career in dance photography. The paper hadn't previously been running pictures of dance along with their reviews but it was changing owners and the new editors had begun to look for visual material. So I was in the right place at the right time.

I guess I was pretty aggressive, too. I remember telephoning Deborah Jowitt, the dance critic, on the recommendation of a mutual friend in Boston, and Deborah told me I was free to photograph the subject of her next article, Laura Dean. So I did, but later Deborah admitted to me that she thought I was very brash.

WAE Before we delve any further into your own work, can we talk about the requirements of your professional dance photography, because, even with your disclaimer, this side to your work does exist, and more importantly, what you are doing today grew out of it.

LG I approach things very differently from the conventional dance photographer, who often has the choreographer arrange the dancers in poses. I hate poses. When I work professionally I strive for two things: first, to make a powerful image and, second, not to misrepresent the choreographer's work. But I do try to be true to the spirit if not the letter of the choreography. However, these two things are by no

Daniel Ezralow sheds conventions along with his clothes in much of his collaborative work with Greenfield, whose approach calls for total spontaneity on the part of the dancers. (See also Plate 58.)

means necessarily connected. A great piece of choreography will not necessarily make a great photograph. Neither will a great dancer.

WAE You say that dance photographers work from poses. But what about those who attend performances or dress rehearsals?

LG At the beginning I functioned that way. But I found working during performances too nerve-wracking. There I was, clicking away incessantly and disturbing people who had paid a considerable amount of money to enjoy the program. Yet I still had to come back with a great shot.

So I gave that up and tried dress rehearsals, but they're not ideal either. First of all the dancers are not always fully costumed. And what's the use of a photograph of Gelsey Kirkland and Mikhail Baryshnikov if Kirkland's wearing chunky leg warmers? No magazine would print it. Also, the dancers are not always performing full out—to a certain extent they're just going through the motions. And then the lighting will continually change throughout the piece—if one is lucky enough even to *have* enough light.

WAE It must also be frustrating to have no control over the event. It unfolds according to the choreographer's agenda, not the photographer's, and you have to catch it as best you can. I suppose it has a hit or miss quality, like reportage.

LG And, just when you have everything right, another photographer might pop up in front of you as he or she jockeys for the best angle. You should see the contraptions my colleagues would set up!—four cameras each, equipped with different lenses and loaded with a variety of films, all jerryrigged on tripods—they were ready for anything. Or you might be changing your film just as Baryshnikov executes that spectacular leap!

It was these obstacles which pushed me to get my own studio where I could exercise control. This I did in 1980. And more and more dancers came to my studio. Now I'd go to theaters only under duress. My assignments for the *Voice* brought fifty-two dancers or groups into my studio each year—a new challenge every week. And the *Voice* encouraged me to make each of them look different. So not only did I have to differentiate one dancer's, or one choreographer's, work from the next, I had to make, say, Laura Dean's *new* dance look clearly different from her *old* one.

WAE In retrospect, the *Voice*'s insatiable appetite seems to have provided an extraordinary opportunity, a kind of experimental photo laboratory for you.

LG The challenge certainly provoked a more critical and analytical approach on my part. Remember, I felt a certain distance from the dance world. I was an outsider. Rather than being an awe-struck fan, worshipping the dance with my camera, I was an objective viewer asking the dance to astonish me. Nor did I assume that my pictures were going to have a captive audience, but felt that I had to compete with the mass of visual imagery which bombards us daily, that I had to grab the reader's attention as he or she flipped through the pages of the *Voice*.

WAE And how was this to be accomplished?

LG By looking for, and hopefully identifying, the kernel of uniqueness in the choreography or the dancer's personal style, and giving that kernel form and substance.

WAE I can understand this in general or metaphorical terms, but perhaps you can be more specific?

LG When you break a dance into its components a lot of the movements are either from standard dance vocabulary, or they are gestures and movements common to many people's work, even if they are reassembled or reworked in other ways. So when these movements are isolated as fragments they do not necessarily reveal the uniqueness of the dancer. And the situation becomes even more difficult now when I see the descendants of the people I photographed in 1973 or '75. Let's say, for example, that Diane Madden, a dancer who has worked with Trisha Brown, comes to my studio because the *Voice* is reviewing her own choreography. I don't want the picture to look as if it's one of Diane performing Trisha. I want to do justice to Diane's originality. This is complicated by the fact that, quite naturally, Diane's body and her way of moving have been shaped by years of working with Trisha. But because I have a good memory and a great deal of experience, I know her artistic roots and therefore I know what to eliminate.

WAE So it's a matter of deciding first what to dispose of?

LG Yes. It's like chipping away at marble to arrive eventually at the sculpture. I chip away all the things I don't want and I'm left with only a few that I do. Diane will show me something, and I'll reject it. She'll try something else, and I'll reject that too. But then the next thing may be something that I have never seen before, something that reveals her kinesthetic originality, her unique dance personality.

WAE I can certainly see why you would want—need—your own studio. Your preferred way of working is highly collaborative. Is this why you're attracted to modern and postmodern forms as opposed to ballet?

LG Yes. Take Trisha Brown, for instance. In our very earliest sessions she'd run solos for me and I would make Polaroids. When I showed her the Polaroids, something extraordinary happened. She didn't recognize her own choreography! Why? Because I was photographing transitional moments, moments between two peaks, rather than the peaks themselves. So I was unwittingly showing her a new facet of her work. Now with ballet, the photographic moments are either right or wrong: Makarova is either on point or not. What attracted me to modern and postmodern—let's call it experimental—dance, was that it was composed of equally valid moments. Given a certain level of competence most dance photographers would emerge from a dress rehearsal of the American Ballet Theater's production of *Coppelia* or *Sleeping Beauty*, say, with very similar moments. The only differentiating characteristics, if any, would be whether the moment was taken from the right or left side of center. But with experimental dance I'd often find, in comparing contact sheets with a colleague, that it was hard to believe we'd been shooting the same event. I'm referring here, of course, to those dreaded dress rehearsals. But at least they taught me how much creative latitude a photographer really had with postmodern and experimental dance and I was heartened to realize that I could be more than a mere recordmaker.

WAE Once you had your own studio, and could exert control over the photographic event, what did you make of it?

LG It encouraged me to think about the medium of photography on its own terms, to develop its unique attributes. I realized that although people are used to seeing carefully crafted images which glorify the dance, these pictures don't tell you anything more; they don't develop, extend, explore. People would look at one of my pictures of Baryshnikov in a spectacular leap ten feet off the ground and say, "What a great photograph!", but I knew that it wasn't; it was merely a great dance moment competently captured. So I decided to be more exploratory. In the late seventies, for instance, I began to experiment with time exposures, but not just for pretty effects—the overworked "artistic" blur—but to reveal patterns and structures that were invisible to the naked eye.

WAE Because they happen too fast for the eye to register?

LG Yes and no. You see, I didn't want to capture the thin slice of the split second, but to play with the elastic notion of the stretched moment. I had seen Michael Moschen—who was virtually reinventing the art of juggling—perform a solo swinging a lighted torch as a prelude to a dance concert. I was intrigued by the idea of how this could be transformed by photography. So the images I made were uniquely photographic events. In performance you'd have seen a complete circle of fire, but I was able to do quarter circles, or half circles.

WAE As you developed these ideas did you find that there were limitations, or new obstacles in your path?

LG Well, for one thing, I wasn't used to directing what was happening in front of the camera. I first had to recall the parts of the dance that had initially attracted me,

In this 35mm study of Michael Moschen, Greenfield's intention was to use photography to extend vision. Her interest at the time of its making (1978) was the notion of a *stretched*, rather than "split," second. Later, Greenfield would abandon 35mm for the square format $2\frac{1}{4}''$ camera.

communicate these to the dancer, and then reposition the dancers and condense their placements and movements to fit my frame. I also had to redesign certain gestures, so they read more clearly. To give a simple example, I'd have to tell a dancer to keep her arm from blocking her face when she jumped.

WAE Was lighting also a new problem?

LG It was one thing to complain about bad lighting in the theater—now I had to invent my own. I certainly didn't want to duplicate theatrical lighting in my studio the way some photographers do. In fact I was trying to distance myself as much as I could from the theatrical esthetic. And I had a technical problem to solve too—I had to develop a lighting system that would give me the directional light I like, sweeping across a 20-foot space, *without* shadowing the bodies of the dancers— often as many as twelve.

WAE Can you describe the studio set-up without being overly technical? I think it is astonishing, for example, that these often, shall we say, explosive dance images which seem to occupy limitless space are in fact crafted in what is in effect a box some twelve feet wide and high and maybe twenty feet deep. Your studio, with all its props and accoutrements, is of course much bigger, but that box is the arena in which the dancers operate.

LG Not to complicate things, but I actually had two studios at different times, and the first of them had what's called a cyclorama, a structure with a back wall which curves out at the base to meet the floor seamlessly. That gave me far more openness and flexibility than the so-called box I have now. That twelve feet of width you've mentioned isn't arbitrary—it's the maximum width of seamless back-drop paper. So it forced me to compress the dancers, and sometimes to crop them. And I realized that I liked those constraints and could work with them. I had to fight to make the dancers fit, and that limitation helped me go beyond the traditional esthetics of dance photography.

WAE This box—to stick with the metaphor for a moment—echoes the square format you've adopted, a format that derives from your use of the Hasselblad camera, with its $2\frac{1}{4}''$ square negative image. You haven't always photographed with a Hasselblad, have you?

LG No, I began with 35mm, which as everybody knows is a rectangular format. You're right about the box echoing the frame, and it's important to know how I came to all this. In 1982 I had borrowed a Hasselblad because I needed it for some bread-and-butter fashion assignments. I decided to try it out on Dave Parsons and Danny Ezralow, two young dancers with the Paul Taylor Dance Company who had come in to be photographed for the *Voice*. Now the camera had a slightly telephoto lens on it, which in effect propelled me forward and savagely limited the field of view. You're looking down into the viewfinder and everything you see is reversed, so bodies actually moving from left to right travel across the screen *right to left*. Initially it's very, very disorienting! But when I made prints the results were startling—those cropped or severed bodies hurtling through space. I knew I was on to something but to tell you the truth I didn't know what. And the $2\frac{1}{4}''$ format did something else for me that was very important. It could sync at a shutter speed of 1/500th of a second, meaning that I had more control over that flash of light, with the result that my pictures were sharper. What it *really* meant was that Dave wouldn't have a blurry foot! Of course, the larger negative also added to that clarity. After this my 35mm material seemed like junk to me and I never used 35mm in the studio again. If the Hasselblad broke down during shooting, I would just end the session rather than pick up the 35.

WAE Chronologically speaking, in terms of your career and development, this discovery was a watershed, marking the start of your mature personal work. But can you make clear how your thoughts were evolving on dance photography *per se*?

LG As I've mentioned, I was enjoying a measure of success by the mid to late seventies. I was submitting pictures to a number of important publications and seeing them published, both in black-and-white and color. But by around 1979 or '80 I was growing restless. I couldn't continue to meet this demand and still develop my personal approach. I suppose I had just had enough of catering to the market.

WAE Ah, but I suspect there was more to it than that. Some more profound dissatisfaction?

LG That's true. I was growing disenchanted with photographing other people's works of art. I didn't want to be just a technician. I wanted to create something which would stand on its own.

Over the years one's standards change. At the very beginning, when I catapulted myself into the dance world, I was happy to get any recognizable image at all, especially in a dark theater. Then by 1976 I had learned to pre-visualize which parts would work out. I could identify the peak moments and anticipate them. But then I began to think "peak moment photography" was merely a form of target practise. But I had to go through each stage in turn to get where I am now.

WAE There is another side of you, of your work, and that is your writing about photography. I would like to ask you that inescapable question about "influences" now, because I think the two areas are closely interrelated. When you began working as a photographer, what did you know? Who was important to you?

LG I suppose there are two parts to the answer—the first has to do with what I knew about photography when I first began as a photojournalist, and the second, when I entered the field of the dance. In the first instance, I must admit, I didn't know very much. I knew something about the major photographers, such as Cartier-Bresson, Kertész and Lartigue, but very little about people like Muybridge or Marey, whose early studies of movement now interest me. I was familiar with Harold Edgerton, and his famous stop-action photography, but it all seemed so scientific. But what I knew or didn't know wasn't a reflection of my interest—I just hadn't had much exposure. But I remember making a trip to the Bibliothèque Nationale when I was in Paris once, to see the work of Nadar, and that same summer I interviewed Jacques-Henri Lartigue.

WAE Come to think of it, there's an astonishing parallel between the work of Lartigue and your own. I once asked him how he managed to catch his friends and relatives doing all those outlandish jumps and pratfalls and he replied, "Oh, it was simple, I tripped him," or "I pushed her." In other words, he wasn't just the quick-witted observer which everyone had assumed him to be. He intervened and made events happen, as you do.

LG Well, I didn't know that. But you've certainly struck on something! I wanted to write about him partly because of the freshness and spontaneity of his work. In fact, you could hardly call it work! He was just having fun with that new invention that let him sneak up on ladies in the Bois de Boulogne. And as it's always been movement which has attracted me, I guess what you say makes sense.

Now if we jump ahead to my beginnings in dance photography, I'd have to confess to ignorance again. What I did see as I went along didn't interest me because so much of it was so stylized, static and posed. But one also has to remember that there wasn't a history of dance photography at that time—your own, *The Fugitive Gesture*, was the first, and that did not appear until 1987.

WAE That's true. But to get back to your writing, if I'm not mistaken it was going on just about the time you were beginning your dance work in '73 or thereabouts, and, more importantly, the process appears to have been truly inspiring.

LG Hugely inspirational. The first of my articles was on Diane Arbus, whose work I had seen at the Museum of Modern Art in New York. Her photographs frightened and intrigued me and I wanted to discover why. It occurred to me, among many other dimensions of her work that probably aren't relevant to our discussion, that her photographs together constituted a theater, with her subjects the actors. The

An effective illusion of balance was the goal in this game involving the third of Greenfield's foremost collaborators, Ashley Roland, here joined by Daniel Ezralow and Jamey Hampton. (See also Plate 67.)

acute detail, such as vivid moles and pores, seemed to lend an *un*reality to the image, which is the reverse of what one would expect. I also liked the way she transformed the idea of pictorial composition. Instead of a formal quality, it had to do with brightness, quietness, and even mistakes. Sometimes a picture's "wrongness" made it right.

I later wrote on Duane Michals—whose outlook has had a profound effect on me—on Man Ray and on Lucas Samaras, all photographers who invent, rather than depict.

WAE Yes, I recall your quote from Breton in your piece on Man Ray: ". . . the pilot of the never seen, shipwrecker of the predictable." Again and again in your writings you voice this fascination with accident, chance, free association, dream. But what specifically was it about Michals' work that appealed to you so greatly?

LG As you say, I was drawn to the way he made the unexpected happen in his photographs, such as having people gradually dissolve into blurs. He was more interested in the emotional resonance of an event than in the event itself. He didn't rely on the fixed moment—he would integrate the present with the past, juxtapose the dream with the reality and speculate on the future at the same time.

It was actually as much his philosophy as his work that inspired me. When I was in college I went to hear him speak at Massachusetts Institute of Technology. In this iconoclastic lecture he said to a crowd of Minor White/zone system enthusiasts, "If all your life means to you is water running over rocks, then photograph it, but I want to create something that would not have existed without me." Voilà.

WAE You also wrote very favourably on two *dance* photographers at about this time, Barbara Morgan and Max Waldman. What did you see in their work?

LG With Morgan, several things. I liked the way she was able to work with costume so as to reveal movement—*Letter to the World* is a good example, with the skirt's swirl making manifest the preceding movement of the leg—and also the depth of her collaboration with her dancers, especially Martha Graham. I remember telling Morgan during her interview that I saw her double exposures, or montages, which showed different aspects of the dance in the same frame, as, in effect, her own choreography. She would test the compositional strength of her photographs by turning them upside down as she believed a good pictorial structure will work from any viewpoint. So you can see certain seeds were being sown in my mind!

WAE There are other seeds which should be noted as well: you said, and I quote, "Morgan's genius was her ability to dissect movement into its emotional anatomy. Merce Cunningham, in *Leap*, strides through space as though gravity were a figment of someone else's imagination." Yet this observation might apply as well to your own work. And Max Waldman?

LG I wrote a piece on Max called *Dwelling in Texture*, which had of course to do with that heavy grain which characterized his style. This grain was very effective as a dramatic element. It was as if his actors and dancers could not extricate themselves from it.

Not only did he inspire me but he gave me confidence. He rarely opened his studio to other photographers, fearing his secrets might be stolen, but he did to me, which was very trusting. And in 1979 he encouraged me to pursue my own vision and subordinate the newspaper work, just as he had abandoned commercial activity.

WAE He was a real mentor, then. But you didn't exactly go off and extend Waldman's vision.

LG No, but I did develop an equivalent, if you will, of his potent device of grain—the concept of the frame as both a physical boundary or limit and a suggestion of a world just outside it, apart yet connected. My frame, like his grain, exerts a physical force on the dancers.

I should also mention another influence Max's example has been on my work. Recently I have been moving away from strict formalism and pure movement and working for an emotional and dramatic context for the figures. This harks back to Max's work. He often alluded to classical themes, as, for example, in a series after Masaccio which dealt with the expulsion from Paradise, and in fact this work to some extent prefigured a series I'm working on now (Plates 3–9).

WAE Which brings us to your collaborators, the dancers themselves. And first and foremost are Dan and Dave—Daniel Ezralow and David Parsons. When did this collaboration begin, and how did it develop?

LG I actually met Dave first. I was photographing him for a *Voice* supplement of 1982 on the ten best dancers of the year, of which he was one. Because I was photographing the *dancer* rather than the dance, he was free to improvise—to float or to dive, for example—and I thought, "Wow," he really has something. It was a combination of athleticism and lyricism. The visual theme of the *Voice* supplement was a long shot of the studio, so you saw Dave against the white paper but you also saw the flats, props, lights and general paraphernalia. Now, if the shots had been traditionally cropped and in-close, you would have had the illusion of that white paper going on forever. There would have been an implied infinity. I decided I wanted to develop this.

The next time, Dave came with Danny, and the two of them started jumping around, and I had to admire their tremendous energy, their try-anything spirit. In a sense we were very unlikely collaborators. Dave, as I've said, was a Paul Taylor dancer, and Taylor's choreography didn't develop those transitional moments I gravitated towards. And Danny was soon to leave Paul Taylor and join Momix, an offshoot of Pilobolus, and, like Pilobolus, acrobatic and gymnastic. So we were coming from different worlds in a way. Dan and Dave were just starting to discover how their bodies moved independently of choreography. And I felt like an amateur behind this new camera I had borrowed. Danny described himself as a piece of clay which he would throw up in the air to make a different shape each time. The dancer was being liberated from the dance! They had no preconceptions as to *how* they should look. We trusted each other and were free to fail.

WAE Why do you say "free to fail" and not "free to experiment," or "free to succeed"?

LG I took a course with Lisette Model, a famous teacher at the New School, and she used to talk about "the magnificent failure," that is, the picture that tried for a way of seeing beyond the conventional modes which were assured of an easy success. That's part of it. But also, I suppose I mean that we *all* had nothing to lose. We didn't *have* to get results. So each of us was privately saying, "This doesn't really count." So we had no inhibitions.

I have to confess that it was like kindergarten. It might sound corny but it really did feel as if we were toys which came to life when the toymaker went to sleep. Because in fact we did work at night, and by day they were respectable dancers with fine companies and I was this serious professional doing various assignments. But at night the toys played! We played with mirrors, clothes, available props, even babies! I felt as if I had regained the vision of a child.

WAE How often could you get together like this, while the toymaker slept? Once a week?

LG Oh no! At first we just worked a couple of times a year because of their tour schedule, but recently we've been connecting a lot more.

WAE Another important addition to Dan and Dave was Ashley Roland, who danced with Dan at Momix. How did her entry affect the dynamics of the duo?

LG At first I was reluctant to have Ashley alter the chemistry, as I feared she well might. I thought that two heterosexual men as partners was a dynamite idea. I've always believed the traditional male/female relationships in dance to be very played out, very sentimental. A non-erotic relationship, more on the lines of a sibling rivalry, seemed to me to be just what the world needed! When I added Ashley I worried that we'd somehow end up with a conventional love story implied, a love triangle. But my fears immediately proved groundless. Ashley was a female equivalent of Danny.

WAE Perhaps next down the list of collaborators is the Bill T. Jones/Arnie Zane Company. How do you work with them?

LG Bill T. Jones and his partner Arnie Zane, who died a few years ago, were wonderful collaborators. They put themselves completely in my hands. Arnie was a photographer as well, so he knew enough to leave me to my own devices. Like Dan and Dave they had open minds and would try anything. One of the images we're showing here is a case in point (Plate 69). But before I tell you about it, I have to say it's *not* a typical example of the way I work, which usually relies more on a spontaneous approach, as I've said, but it serves well as an example of collaboration. We began with one dancer who is just out of frame. He was holding on to a sprinkler on the ceiling and standing on a ladder. An assistant you don't see was holding up another dancer's legs. And Bill T. was set to jump off a stool. So, when I gave the signal, the ladder was yanked out, the assistant let go of the legs, Bill T. jumped with his body in that arc-like shape, the girl flung herself across the cyclorama. And we did it twelve times before I felt confident that all the elements had come together—their movements and *my* timing, though you never know until you've seen the contact sheets. The paradoxical fact is that when you're looking through the camera you see everything but the instant when you actually click the shutter—in that

This series of photographs was one of the earliest in which Greenfield was determined to compose fully for the $2\frac{1}{4}''$ camera. The dance shown was not an actual piece of choreography but one invented solely for Greenfield's camera. It was later given the title, *Freedom of Information.*

instant the viewfinder is perfectly blank. More generally, they were the first company to come to me with choreography that they were willing to abandon. That's when I realized that from here on, when I wasn't forced to work to the choreographer's agenda, I would ask my dancers to leave their choreography at the door!

WAE You've certainly explained your penchant for modern/postmodern modes of dance. But occasionally you do ballet. Do you have favorites in this area?

LG The Eliot Feld Ballet is definitely a favorite. I like the fact that they do things in a different way—for example, Feld was more interested in the transitional moments than ballet people normally are. His dancers might take a peak moment and extend it, and this relates to my own notion of the elastic or stretched moment. But it isn't always easy and sometimes I've just had to admit defeat. They were here recently doing a piece in which the moment was exceptionally violent, but the pictures came out looking lyrical—totally wrong! We tried to overcome this with lighting; if you shroud the dancers in shadow, the action automatically takes on ominous tones.

Feld also has an inventive concept of partnering which appeals to me whereby the women slip under, around and through the men in a continuous sweep rather than being supported in an arabesque or *penché*.

WAE I think you could tell a great story for each of the images you've chosen for the book. But what interests me specifically is how you can on occasion appropriate the role of the choreographer. You have crossed the line as it's conventionally drawn and actually involved yourself in the choreography itself. Isn't this so?

LG Yes. For example, Pilobolus recently came to me with a request for what we might call generic Pilobolus photographs—in other words, of no specific works. They're a gymnastically oriented group and I began to direct them in acts of balance and off-balance. I asked Jude Woodcock to jump in such a way that she would appear to be hanging suspended from the other dancer, thus balancing the human construction visually (Plate 72), though not truly physically. I was trying for effects that would disorient the viewer, trying to make things look impossible by providing contradictory information, or clues, as to what is up or down, in motion or still, on or off balance. But these images don't represent anything you will actually see them perform.

WAE Another important collaborator has been Elizabeth Streb. There seems to be a deep affinity here.

LG There is indeed. She's another person whose work relies on daring physicality, and, like me, she loves to work with contradictory forces. And she likes the chaotic, whirlwind quality of thrown things, like the balls (Plate 54), just as I enjoy having objects thrown around. In many ways her work is the choreographic analog to my own. One of the main things she's interested in is the tension between full-out energy and confinement. My dancers are bounded only conceptually by my frame, but her dancers actually throw themselves—splat!—against free-standing walls. Elizabeth's movement is based on the laws of momentum: once you put something in motion it doesn't stop until an outside force stops it. As she puts it, "It's not that we're hitting the wall, it's that the wall is stopping us." She's eliminated a perspective based on vertical bodies. As often as not her dancers are upside down or

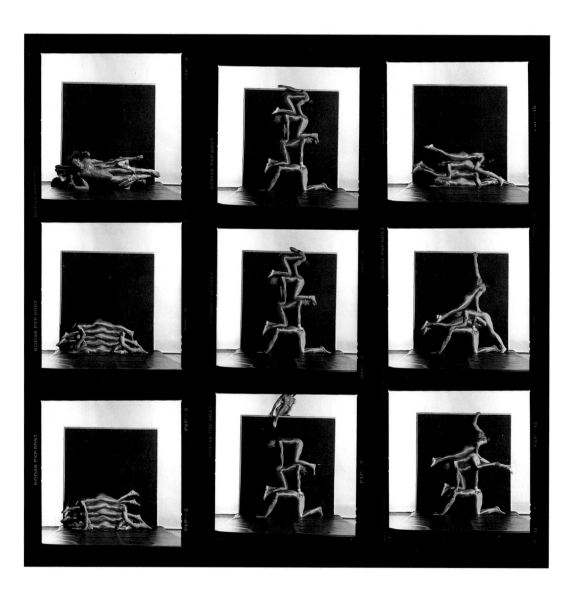

Elizabeth Streb's fascination with contained space, as in *Wall*, 1991, is of great interest to Greenfield, whose own efforts are much concerned with confinement and release.

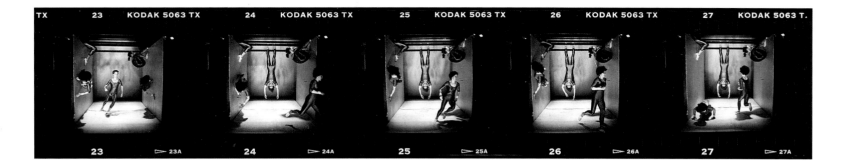

The box constructed by Elizabeth Streb for *Rebound*, 1990, is the perfect analog of Greenfield's frame.

horizontal. Her "Which end is up?" quality is even more startling when it is performed live. I always have to fight the suspicion—entirely unfounded—that I have tricked the viewer photographically.

Am I allowed an aside? People come up with the funniest, most outlandish theories as to how I've taken some of my pictures—the dancers are lying on the ground, they're held up with wires, they're stripped in as montage!—yet, photographically speaking, there are no strings attached, they're just straightforward snapshots!

WAE With the important qualification that you have masterfully prepared the ground. It doesn't mean that anyone standing beside you could take that same snapshot.

LG True, but technically they're still snapshots. Anyway . . . Elizabeth says she builds physical structures or sets not to limit space but to define and question it. Sometimes her choreography, as in *Float*, happens in the split second between a leap and a landing from a fifteen-foot scaffold. Or within the confines of a box she can't even stretch out in. In *Rebound* the set is a 3-dimensional plywood cube eight by eight feet that these dancers must work within or against. The score is an amplification of actual sounds of the dancers as they pound the walls with their bodies. The crashing thuds and cracks of the people against the vibrating structure emphasize how much their energy is intensified by physical compression. It's as though x amount of energy will double or triple in inverse proportion to the size of the container. In my medium of photography, I'm working with similar ideas, but more as an illusionist, my camera providing the same interaction of energy to matter.

WAE As I've written elsewhere about your work, the square format—analog as you say to Streb's box—allows you to dispense with gravity. The four sides are equal in weight—unlike the bottom-heavy 35mm format—so that each side exerts the same gravitational pull on the dancers, all the more so since there are often no other clues as to up or down.

LG And I'm asking you to take my square *literally* as a boundary, not just as an arbitrary window on infinity. So now you've got the dancers butting their heads and brushing limbs against it, or hanging onto it, or being pulled off it. There's a force, as it were, that surrounds the frame that's affecting them, and it's something other than the usual conception of gravity.

WAE Where do you see your work heading?

LG Until a couple of years ago I was just concerned with getting the work seen, getting it published, exhibited, whatever. Then I said to myself, "Oh my God, I'm just recycling the same fifteen pictures to every publication. And it bothered me to see all these magazines with the same work from '82 or '83. It's a fact that some photographers' careers are made with the same twenty-five or thirty pictures taken fifty years earlier but I didn't want to end up like that. It made me realize that I couldn't stand still . . .

And one of the areas I wanted to explore had to do with time and timelessness. In most photographs one luxuriates in the moment presented. You don't look at a Diane Arbus or a Walker Evans and say, "I wonder what was happening a second or a split second earlier?" But because of the seeming *impossibility* of what my dancers are doing you can't help asking yourself, "Where are they coming from? Where are they going?" Or even, "How is he going to land without breaking his neck?" It intrigues me that in 1/500th of a second I can allude to past and future moments even if these are only imagined.

WAE But this is something you've been developing throughout the eighties. It isn't new.

LG Oh yes, it's been an evolving concern. What's new is the construction of a physical frame to represent the camera frame, which Dave dances through and around. I constructed a six-by-six foot plywood frame which was painted black to simulate the black border on my prints—that is, the boundaries of the image as seen through my square format camera (Plates 84–87). With the wooden frame I took this conceptual frame and made it literal.

WAE A frame within a frame . . . and the camera frame is true at one level and false, or an illusion, at another, and conversely the wooden frame is false at one level and true, or real, at another.

Your obsession with gravity, with these elemental forces, often reminds me of contemporary astrophysics, at least as a layman can grasp all that profoundly mysterious stuff about big bangs and black holes.

LG Ah, then I must tell you about a recent experience. I put a slide show together the other day and it contained that portrait of me with Dan and Dave where I'm jumping while holding the camera release and snapping the shutter at the peak of my jump. When my son Alex saw the picture, he said, "Gee, Mom, I love that portrait but I wish that cord wasn't showing." And I said, "Oh, that's the cable release and it shows that I'm the one who's taking the picture!", to which he replied, "Can't you hide the cord and just tell people that it's a self-portrait? Wouldn't they believe you?" And I had to admit that they probably would. But that started me thinking, "Why do I love that cord so much? Is it because it's an umbilical cord? No! I hate that metaphor. I'm *not* attached to my camera. I don't *run* around with it. The only time I carry it is on trips, to photograph my kids like any ordinary parent. But the next revelation to hit me was this . . . it's like the cord of an astronaut, allowing him—or should I say her—to leave the space-capsule, tethered to the "craft" yet free-floating in space for the purpose of exploration. So I like that astrophysical thought of yours—breaking out of the earthly sphere.

WAE Breaking bounds!—it's certainly a metaphor which does justice to your work.

ACKNOWLEDGMENTS

THE PICTURES IN THIS BOOK represent my second decade as a photographer and are the outgrowth of my relationship with two very special dancers, Daniel Ezralow and David Parsons, who, along with Ashley Roland, have been my constant muses over the past ten years. Their extraordinary talent, spontaneous energy and intuitive communication with me have given form and life to my ideas.

Over these years, Jack Deaso has lent his keen eye to all my pictures, enhancing every aspect of my work, from lighting the dancers on the set to printing the images, always noticing the important details that everyone else overlooked.

Chris Karitevlis, with his superb organizational ability and flair for presentation, contributed his energy and ideas to all aspects of the project from darkroom to publisher.

I would also like to thank Douglas Dugan who, along with Chris and Jack, provided beautiful prints for this book.

I owe a great deal to dance critic Deborah Jowitt and my editor Burt Supree of the *Village Voice* in which many of these photographs originally appeared. Their loyalty and enthusiasm have kept my pictures appearing weekly for almost twenty years.

In causing me to reflect more analytically on my work, the discerning critical comments of my husband Stuart Liebman have helped to focus my conceptual energy and have strengthened my vision.

My sons Alex and Jesse taught me that you invent your own world by questioning your perceptions and hypothesizing answers, thereby making the possible more meaningful than the real.

Finally, I wish to express my deep appreciation to Bill Ewing who conceived of, curated, and shaped this book. Just as good dances do not always make good photographs, Bill understood that an interesting book is not just a collection of good pictures. Indeed, after countless designs, layouts, and sequences of images, Bill has given this body of my work its own special choreography.

Lois Greenfield

My thanks to the friends and colleagues who supported my efforts to finally realize a book which has been in my head for more than ten years. I owe a longstanding debt of gratitude to Cornell Capa of the International Center of Photography who first encouraged me to look closely at the field of dance photography in 1978, the result being a major historical exhibition in which Lois's work played a significant part. Her work was first brought to my attention by my curatorial assistant Ruth Silverman, who returned one day from one of her scouting expeditions with a box of photographs which lifted the spirits of those of us who were beginning to think that contemporary dance photography was a lost cause.

Poyin Auyeung's insights into the shortcomings of interview and introduction have, I believe, strengthened both. Lois's assistants, Jack Deaso and Chris Karitevlis, were a pleasure to work with and offered intelligent advice on all aspects of the project. John Heward and Sylvia Safdie were most generous with their spacious loft, where I was able to spread out many hundreds of prints in order to view them simultaneously.

Above all, however, I wish to thank Lois herself, who proved a wonderful partner in the endeavour and a highly articulate advocate of her ideas. From start to finish the project was a deeply satisfying experience.

William A. Ewing

INDEX

Numbers in **bold** refer to plates, numbers in italic to in-text illustrations